The Five Defective Teachers and Staff

Alvin Allen; Dominique Bennett

authorHOUSE®

AuthorHouse™
1663 Liberty Drive
Bloomington, IN 47403
www.authorhouse.com
Phone: 1 (800) 839-8640

Published by AuthorHouse   02/23/2017

ISBN: 978-1-5246-7342-0 (sc)
ISBN: 978-1-5246-7341-3 (e)

Library of Congress Control Number: 2017902738

Print information available on the last page.

Any people depicted in stock imagery provided by Thinkstock are models, and such images are being used for illustrative purposes only. Certain stock imagery © Thinkstock.

This book is printed on acid-free paper.

Because of the dynamic nature of the Internet, any web addresses or links contained in this book may have changed since publication and may no longer be valid. The views expressed in this work are solely those of the author and do not necessarily reflect the views of the publisher, and the publisher hereby disclaims any responsibility for them.

CONTENTS

INTRODUCTION

While at a book review, I met a second-year teacher. She asked me a stimulating question. She said she was very intrigued by one of my previous books. She was curious to know how I knew so much about teachers and students since I only taught for ten years. She researched my career and pondered my success in the classroom and as a consultant. I summed up the key to my success for her in two words: *hard work*! Growing up as an African American male in a rough neighborhood and in a single-parent home were already three strikes against me. I had to witness some things in my environment that no child should witness. This is when I made a promise to myself to be successful! I was determined to be successful, and I want everyone around me to be successful too. In my quest for success, I researched many philosophers and consulted with many of my peers when I first started teaching. I received a number of great ideas over the years, in which I tweaked with my own to development strategies based on my students to reach success. I did not have overnight gratification, but I always was determined to better my craft and to be a lifelong learner and teacher. The young lady looked at me as I spoke and seemed to grasp every word I was saying.

She asked me one last question: "Since you have owned and worked at iLegacy Educational Consulting Firm, is there any school that stood out among the rest?"

I told her, "Yes, Capers Middle School!"

She asked, "Why?"

I asked her, "Have you ever met a defective teacher?" She wasn't sure. I told her, "Well, sit back and relax because this will be a long and interesting lesson."

The Faculty Meeting

I remember the day I received the phone call from Patrick, one of my eldest friends. I hadn't heard from him in over five years. He had been a principal for over ten years in Metropolitan Atlanta. He was transferred to the infamous Capers Middle School to reform the school. This was his third year at Capers Middle, and it wasn't going in the right direction. He wanted me to come to the school and evaluate his staff to see how I could help. I requested a synopsis of his staff and school data for background knowledge. He stated that he would like me to come visit his faculty meeting on the following Tuesday, and afterward he would give me the synopsis. I agreed to attend the faculty meeting.

The meeting was at 3:30 p.m. in the professional development room. It was already 3:15, and no staff was present. At about 3:20, I noticed two teachers had arrived. It was an older woman and a young lady. As I was listening to their conversation, I figured the older woman was a veteran teacher, and she was giving advice to the younger lady. I guess the younger lady was a new teacher or was early in her career.

At 3:30 two other teachers entered and sat in the corner off to themselves. I could tell they were from another country. They were speaking their native language. They had looks of distress on their faces.

Finally at 3:40, before the meeting started, a teacher walked in full of grace. She came into the room, telling everyone hello. You could hear some of the staff whispering negative comments about her. One person said she didn't want to hear anything about her stats or how she was such a great teacher. They offered her fake smiles and said hello in return.

Already, I had noticed problems with the atmosphere of Patrick's school. The faculty weren't punctual, and the relationships were minuscule. Finally at 3:55, Patrick stood up in the front of the room to start the meeting. While he was welcoming the staff to the meeting, a young man entered the room. He was dropping papers and looked disoriented. He was a nervous wreck. He told the principal he was sorry about being late.

A couple of the staff members were laughing at him. During the staff meeting, some staff were on their phones or their laptops, and they look unconcerned with the information being presented in the meeting. Most of the staff were looking at the data and had a nonchalant attitude. I overheard someone say, "This is Capers. What did he expect—good scores?"

The teachers at the table started laughing. The foreign teachers looked confused with the power point presentation. The teacher who came in late was checking papers, working on his laptop, and trying to be attentive all at the same time.

After the meeting, the principal asked me what I thought. I smiled and told him to send me the synopsis ASAP and we would start first thing in the morning.

When I got home, I didn't have time to read the principal's synopsis of his school, but from the faculty meeting, I had enough material to get started. The faculty all worked in the same school building but did not work as a team. They did not operate as one cohesive unit. The staff had "I syndrome." I knew I had to help the staff come together as one to move the school forward, but first I had to work with the five different types of teachers he had on his staff: the foreign teacher, the boastful teacher, the veteran teacher, the new teacher, and the nervous wreck teacher.

After talking, Patrick and I developed a plan to assist his staff. Our number one goal was to bring his staff together to work as a well-oiled machine. My first step in accomplishing this goal was to evaluate some of his teaching staff on a more personal level. We developed a list: Mr. Jenkins (unorganized teacher), Mrs. Robertson (boastful teacher), Ms. Humphrey (the veteran), Ms. Simpson (newbie), and Mrs. Clemente (international teacher).

Meeting the Veteran

Anyone who stops learning is old,
whether at twenty or eighty. Anyone
who keeps learning stays young.

—Henry Ford

Ms. Humphrey had been working at Capers Middle School for twenty years. She'd seen the rise and fall of the school. She had taught every subject at the school, from English to physical education. For the last five years, she had been teaching US history. Mrs. Humphrey had three years left before she would be able to fully retire. She was a religious woman and loved to lend a helping hand to the younger teachers.

When I walked into Mrs. Humphrey's class, the students were quietly doing bell work. It looked like a scene from a well-written movie. I wondered, *Did she warn the students a visitor would come today?* Mrs. Humphrey was walking around the classroom monitoring the students, letting her presence be known.

Once the bell work was over, Mrs. Humphrey called on two students for their answers. For the next forty-five minutes, the students took notes on US history while Mrs. Humphrey lectured the class. During the lecture, you could have heard a pin drop on a ball of cotton. One aspect of the class stood out to me. Even though the classroom was equipped with four desktop computers and a smart board, and each student had his or her own laptop, there was not any technology utilized in her classroom. She did not even use the smart board to write.

She talked and talked. At one moment in the class, a student asked to sharpen her pencil. Mrs. Humphrey looked at the student and pointed to the rules. Rule 3: Students should bring two pencils to class and have the pencils sharpened prior to the start of the lesson. One of the student's peers handed her a pencil. For the last ten minutes of class, Mrs. Humphrey reviewed the notes. The students who missed any key vocabulary on the quick check were assigned homework to write the definition of the words twenty-five times.

This was traditional teaching at its worst and—I might add—boring. Once the class left, Mrs. Humphrey walked over to me with confidence and asked me if I'd enjoyed her lesson. I gave her a smile and stated that her class reminded me of my old US history class. I also commended her on her classroom management. I told Mrs. Humphrey that I would talk to her during her planning to go over the notes I had taken from her class observation.

Mrs. Humphrey's Debriefing

One thing I have learned over the past couple of years is you can't beat around the bush with veteran teachers. They like their feedback straight on the rocks, no chaser. We met in the professional development room for the debriefing. I wanted to meet in a neutral environment that was comfortable for both of us.

Mrs. Humphrey sat down at the table. It is key to always start out with the positives. No teacher will be open to change if you are bashing him or her. First, I told Mrs. Humphrey some good techniques I noticed in her class. I handed her the list.

- She had great classroom management.

- She used proximity (walking around the classroom).

- Students understood the rules and procedures of the class.

- Students were on task throughout the lesson.

- Students had work on the board when they entered the class.

- The teacher did a closure activity.

- There was an outline of the classroom agenda on the board.

She looked at the list and was elated. She told me she was glad that I'd noticed good teaching strategies in her class. I thought, *I also noticed strategies that could be changed for the twenty-first-century learner.* I told Mrs. Humphrey I was impressed by those strategies, and I formed a list to help take her teaching to the next level, I gave her a list of things she could improve.

- implementation of technology

- student-centered activities

- less lecturing

- competition/games

- random selection of students

- differentiate instruction/rotations

She looked at the list and stated she had been teaching twenty-odd years and her style worked. She pulled out pictures of her former students who were successful. I ensured her that I was not bashing her methods. Then I asked her one question: Are the students you teach today like the ones you taught years ago? She looked at me and said no. I let her know my job was to help her to implement new activities to add to her teaching arsenal.

I was not there to just drop off ideas for her class, get my check, and then leave her to fend for herself. I would also help her implement them, if she was willing. She said if I could help her, she was open to learning. Since she was a religious woman, I asked her to pray that we would both learn and grow from each other. Mrs. Humphrey left the room with an open mind, but I knew I had a lot of work to do to adjust her way of teaching.

Next Stop

The Newbie

Children must be taught how to
think, not what to think.

—Margaret Mead

I wanted to observe the new teacher next
because I'd noticed in the faculty meeting
that she and Mrs. Humphrey had a working

relationship. I figured I might be able to use their relationship to my advantage.

Ms. Simpson had just graduated from Francis Marion University. She had a bachelor's degree in early childhood development and a master's degree in mathematics. She had done her student teaching in a rural middle school in South Carolina. Capers Middle School was a totally different environment from what she was used to. Also, this was her first year of teaching.

I arrived in Ms. Simpson's class prior to the bell ringing. I introduced myself to her and told her I was going to observe her class for a few minutes. Ms. Simpson became a little nervous. I reassured her that this was not a formal observation and it would not go in her personnel file. When the students came into the class, they were loud and playful. There didn't seem to be a routine. This was a big difference from Mrs. Humphrey's class. Ms. Simpson spent about five minutes just getting the students to settle down and get on task. Once the students were on task, the students had to log onto their laptops. They went on a site called Edmodo.com. The bell work was on this particular website. The students answered the questions and e-mailed them back to Ms. Simpson. Some of the students completed their assignment quickly and started to watch music videos on their devices. After all, the students were finished with their bell work.

Ms. Simpson had students choose three partners to do their math stations. The students seemed enthusiastic about doing the group activities. Ms. Simpson had four stations. One station was at a table. There were eight problems on a sheet of paper, and the group had to work together to calculate the answers. Ms. Simpson was at the table with the students. She was helping them in a small group capacity.

The second group was in the back of the class. They had a gallery walk activity. There were four different posters on the walls. Three of the posters displayed the four different types of slopes. The fourth poster was an error analysis poster, where students had to identify the error with the given solution. The posters were hand drawn and written. They displayed pictures of various types of slopes using real-life examples. Each of the posters also had informational bullets. The students had to view each of the posters and take notes based on their observations and conclusions they made as a group.

The third station was on their laptops. The students were given a website to visit. On the website, they had to calculate the slope given various representations. The students also had to research the different methods of calculating the slope of a line.

The last station was at the Promethean ActivTable. They had a lazy river activity to complete. They had to place the right slopes in the barrels on the lazy river. Once they placed all the correct slopes in the barrels, the ActiviTable gave them immediate feedback. The students were at each station for ten minutes. The stations were a great student-centered activity, but some of the students did all the work while the others copied. Other students just talked and played from station to station.

Before Ms. Simpson could bring the class back together, the bell rang. The students ran out of the room like they heard a fire alarm. I stayed behind and told Ms. Simpson her activities were excellent and I enjoyed them. I told her I would debrief with her during her planning.

The Newbie

Debriefing

I wanted to meet Ms. Simpson in a different environment than her classroom or the professional development room. I met her in the library. The library was quiet and relaxing. I felt she needed to be in a tranquil place away from all distractions.

When Ms. Simpson entered the library, she had a big smile on her face. She was a very jolly and motivated individual. As a former educator and as a consultant, I have seen teachers start their career off with that same attitude, and after the first two years, they lose all their drive.

When we sat down, I reiterated to Ms. Simpson how much I enjoyed her activities. Remember, the key is to start with the positives. I then asked her how her second month of teaching was going. She stated she had some good days and bad days but she was up for the task of teaching. She said her goal was to help all her kids at the inner city school be successful!

She was not afraid of a challenge. She wanted all her students to be engaged and passionate about learning. I let her know I was impressed with her drive and determination. Like I always do, I gave Ms. Simpson the list of all the great techniques I observed in her classroom.

- Great use of technology

- Differentiated instructions

- Small group learning

- Student-centered classroom

- Students' engagement

Ms. Simpson smiled when she received the list. She stated it was the first time this year someone acknowledged that she was using some great strategies in the classroom. Now I had to give her a list of things to improve.

- Rules and procedures

- Classroom management

- Flex grouping

- Closing activity

- Student accountability

- Routines

Ms. Simpson was very open to my written notes on improvements. She was eager to work with me to improve her weaknesses. She stated, "I requested assistance with these areas previously, but to no advantage." I asked Mrs. Simpson if she had a mentor to really assist her during her first year. She stated, "No, but Mrs. Humphrey assists when she can." I told Ms. Simpson, she would be hearing from me in the next day with some different strategies to strengthen her as a teacher.

The Plan for the Newbie and the Veteran

At the end of the day, I spoke to my friend Patrick. I told him that I visited Mrs. Humphrey's and Ms. Simpson's classes. I told him that I was impressed by some strategies the teachers used. He said he knew he had some great teachers at the school, but he didn't know where the school was falling short.

I asked him if I could have some leeway in helping the teachers on his staff. He said he would not stand in my way. I told him I needed to take Ms. Simpson and Mrs. Humphrey to lunch tomorrow for about two hours off campus. In any relationship bonding is very important. It helps build trust. He was skeptical about the idea, but he agreed to get coverage for their classes for tomorrow.

When I arrived home from Capers Middle, I reviewed my notes. I realized that Mrs. Humphrey's weaknesses were Ms. Simpson's strengths and vice versa. Since Mrs. Humphrey and Ms. Simpson had an established relationship, they would be more open to helping each other.

The next day I met both of the women, walking into the building. I told them I was taking them to lunch today. Ms. Simpson was ecstatic and overjoyed, but Mrs. Humphrey was not elated. She didn't want to miss her class. She said she didn't have a substitute or anything meaningful prepared, and her students would be behind in their work. I assured her that Mr. Dent would have someone watch her class and her students would complete their assignment. After about five minutes, Mrs. Humphrey agreed to go. I let the teachers choose the restaurant for us to eat. Mrs. Humphrey wanted to go to Golden Corral for some soul food.

When we first met for lunch, the atmosphere at the table was tense. I had to find a way to make everyone feel comfortable and break the ice. I asked Mrs. Humphrey how long she had worked at Capers and how many times the school had changed principals since she had been there. She said she had been working there for twenty years and she had been led by more than eight different principals. I asked what was one of the most memorable moments she had while teaching at the school. She told us about the time when one of her former principals and a custodian were fighting in the teacher lounge. She said the principal installed a small camera in the refrigerator to see who was stealing people's lunches. Come to find out, it was one of the custodians. When the principal walked into the teacher lounge, the custodian was eating some of the principal's lunch. He snatched his lunch out of the custodian's hand, and in return the custodian threw a drink on him. Next thing you know, they both were throwing food and punches at each other.

She said, "When we walked in the lounge, it was food all over the place and both of them were out of breath and covered in macaroni and greens. It was a hot mess."

Five minutes after she finished the story, we were all still laughing at the table. That hilarious story was just what I needed to set the tone. Now that everyone was loose and comfortable, I asked Ms. Simpson about the Edmodo site her students used to complete their bell work. She said she used it for bell work and any time the students had to turn in assignments. The work was sent to her, and she was able to correct the assignments and send the students feedback. Mrs. Humphrey said she needed Edmono or Edmundo or whatever you call it in her life so she would not have to take around so much paper and could instantly give her students feedback.

We started laughing hysterically again. Ms. Simpson said she could create her an account and show her how to use it. Ms. Simpson pulled out her laptop and created Mrs. Humphrey an account. I watched in amazement while Ms. Simpson showed her how to use Edmodo. com. I told Ms. Simpson not to show her too much and to just give her the basics so Mrs. Humphrey could utilize it with her bell work. After ten minutes, Mrs. Humphrey was able to create bell work for tomorrow. Mrs. Humphrey stated that she was a new fifty-year-old techie. Mrs. Humphrey wanted to know what types of procedures Ms. Simpson had in place for the usage of the devices and websites. Ms. Simpson stated she did not think about procedures for the use of the device, and before I could chime in, the teachers started to make a list for device usage on Edmodo.

I then told the ladies they should consider this anytime they allowed the students to use the technology. While we were eating, a school bus arrived outside. The students, accompanied by two teachers, walked in the restaurant. The students quietly walked in an orderly fashion. They seemed well-behaved and well-mannered.

Ms. Simpson said, "I wish my kids acted like that just one day of the week."

Before I could say anything, Mrs. Humphrey chimed in. She told Ms. Simpson she needed to have set procedures and routines and consequences for everything in her class. She needed to go over them with each of her classes and make the students actually practice them. She told Ms. Simpson that she had to hold her students accountable for their actions and show consistency. If the students misbehaved during an activity, she should redirect their behavior by restating the rule. If the students continued, give them a different activity named *book work*.

Mrs. Humphrey told Ms. Simpson to stay stern and stand by her procedures and never deviate. Mrs. Humphrey reassured Ms. Simpson that the students' behaviors would eventually change.

I think the lunch meeting was a success. We laughed and joked, and the teachers shared effective strategies with each other. I think the teachers generated a brand new respect for one another. They created a bond where each of them would learn and continuously grow. When lunch was over, I told the teachers that I would be visiting their rooms next week to do a follow up.

Meeting Ms. Boastful

Education is the ability to listen to almost anything without losing your temper or your self-confidence.

—Robert Frost

After having such a great experience with Ms. Simpson and Mrs. Humphrey from Capers Middle School, I was now ready to meet Ms. Boastful. Are you familiar with the type of teacher who brags loudly about all his or her successes but whispers his or her failures? This type of teacher is a know-it-all but different from the veteran know-it-all. Where a veteran has experienced plenty and really knows a lot, the boastful teacher has a taste of success through guidance and believes he or she is on the same status.

Now do not get me wrong, there is nothing wrong with being boastful about your hard work when it is tasteful. When it creates a barrier in the atmosphere that hinders the students from getting the best education possible, something has to change. I entered Mrs. Robertson's class maybe fifteen minutes after the bell. The late entrance was intentional.

She was sitting at her desk, and a student was writing down terms on the board. Before I sat down, a student walked over to me. The student introduced himself as the student ambassador to the class. He pointed out the location of the agenda and their current learning standard in the classroom. He directed me to my seat and handed me the lesson plan book. The students were also reading the novel *The Outsiders*. I was very impressed. Mrs. Robertson's class was a direct example of being student-centered. She had specific students lead the direct instruction and guided practice. Some students were in groups analyzing specific chapters, and other students were at the smart board doing a character analysis. In the back of the classroom, there were four students participating in a read aloud.

Mrs. Robertson walked around with a clipboard and did an informal assessment of the students. To the naked eye, the classroom resembled complete chaos because of all the noise and movement, but it was really a fun and engaging environment. The class was exceptional except for one matter. I saw a girl and boy in the back of the class not doing anything. The boy had his head down, and the girl was playing with her fingernails. I overheard a student ask Mrs. Robertson if they should give them any work. She stated that there was not any hope for them. Then she smiled at the two kids in the back of class.

Alvin Allen; Dominique Bennett

While the students were working in their groups, a boy was whispering to another student next to me. He said that Mrs. Robertson always chose the same people to lead the instruction. Mrs. Robertson referred to them as the "chosen ones." Even though I was impressed by Mrs. Robertson's overall class, she did have one or two deficiencies that I needed to discuss with her. When the class was over, Mrs. Robertson had a break until her next class. She told me she would like to sit down and discuss her observation while she had a break. I usually took time to analyze my notes before I met with a teacher, but I made an exception for her.

The Boastful

Debriefing

Before I could get together my thoughts, Mrs. Robertson started the meeting. For the first ten minutes, she told me about all her statistics over the years. In her first five years, she had been nominated three times for teacher of the year. She had a 85 percent or better passing rate on ELA and reading state standardized test, which was 20 percent higher than the district and the state averages.

Also, she basically stated in so many words that I was wasting my time observing her because she did not need any help. This is where so many teachers and people get it wrong. Every craft can be improved! Nobody but the Almighty himself is perfect. While she was talking about all her accomplishments and milestones, I was contemplating a method in which to talk with her. I started off by acknowledging and complimenting her on all of her successes over her brief teaching career. I asked if she ever considered working at the district level as a consultant. She could share her methods of success. A true leader is able to multiply or make more of him or herself. Mrs. Robertson laughed and asked if I was hiring. I laughed and told her that she was needed here, but she needed to come see in the next five years. I told Mrs. Robertson that her class displayed student engagement and higher-order thinking to the highest degree.

It was fascinating to see the students lead. I told her that most of her students were on task and engaged. Before I could say the next statement, she stopped me.

She had a look of disgust on her face and said, "Most. Please don't count those two in the back of the class. They never do any work. They are on a third-grade reading level. Somebody failed them a long time ago. I can't save everybody."

Since she was such a great teacher, I was shocked by her comment. I told her that she should never give up on her students but fight to the end. It is her duty as a educator to meet them where they are—to teach them something, anything!

Mrs. Robertson became defensive. She stated, "We can agree to disagree when it comes to that topic."

I noticed that the meeting was not going in the right direction, so I told Mrs. Robertson to forgive me, but I needed to go observe Mr. Jenkins's class.

Alvin Allen; Dominique Bennett

Out of all the teachers, I knew Mrs. Robertson would be my biggest challenge. She had already made up in her mind that she was the best and no one could help perfection, but boy was she wrong.

Mr. Jenkins

Mr. Unorganized

Often, it's not about becoming a new
person, but becoming the person
you were meant to be, and already
are, but don't know how to be.

—Heath L. Buckmaster

When I was heading to Mr. Jenkins's class,
someone ran by me like a streak of

lightning. It was Mr. Jenkins. He was trying to get to his class before the tardy bell rang. He was in so much of a hurry that he dropped some of his papers. I picked them up for him since I was heading to his class.

When I walked in the class, Mr. Jenkins was at the board talking to his students. "Boys and girls, have a seat! Now what did I have planned for ya'll today? Oh yeah, that's right, rocks!"

The students did not look puzzled at all by Mr. Jenkins's remark. It seemed to be a regular routine for them. They were all poised and ready to work. Mr. Jenkins was at his cabinet and looking on his desk for something.

While he was searching through a pile of papers, I was shocked to see none of the students off task. I thought they must really respect Mr. Jenkins. Finally, he found a stack of colored papers. Mr. Jenkins handed six students gray paper, seven students blue paper, and six other students beige paper. He told the students to take out their laptops and research the three types related to rocks. He told the students to make mental notes about each of the types of rocks.

After fifteen minutes, Mr. Jenkins told the students with the blue paper to writes notes on the paper pertaining to sedimentary rocks. The students with the beige papers had to write about igneous rocks, and the last group had to write about metamorphic rocks. Each group would be required to present to the class.

The audience would be required to make notes from the presented materials. Mr. Jenkins gave the students twelve minutes to take notes on their specific rock. When the timer rang, the groups were required to present. Mr. Jenkins then informed the students that they would have a rock fight. He told each group to go to a different corner in the room with their notebooks and their colored paper. He gave the students directions for the rock fight.

The students had to ball up their colored paper and throw it at the other groups. Once a person from the other group caught a paper, he or she had to play charades for his or her partner to guess the type of rock he or she caught. The students had so much fun.

After the activity, they came back to their desks and had to collaborate with a partner to explain to different types of rocks as a closing activity. Mr. Jenkins may have been unorganized, but he had a creative and engaging activity planned for his students. The students were so occupied in their learning that they didn't realize the bell was about to ring.

When the bell rang, Mr. Jenkins stood at the classroom door. He asked each student an individual question about rocks. This was the student's ticket to leave. I asked Mr. Jenkins if I could see his lesson plan because I was very impressed by his lesson. He looked through the stacks and stacks of paper on his desk, but he could never find the lesson plan. I told Mr. Jenkins I would meet him before school tomorrow because it was the end of the day.

When I arrived at home, I received a phone call from Patrick. Mrs. Robertson came to see him at the end of the school day. She wanted to the discuss my meeting with her. Patrick said that Mrs. Robertson felt offended and unappreciated after our debriefing. Since Mrs. Robertson had the best scores at the school, she knew Patrick had to keep her on the staff and happy.

I assured him that I did not say or do anything to offend Mrs. Robertson at all. I actually enjoyed her class and wanted to give her some ideas to make it even better. Patrick said Mrs. Robertson could be a bit much to put up with, but she cared a lot about most of her students. That was the second time I heard the word *most* when it came to Mrs. Robertson's and students. I didn't believe Patrick would accept that as an educator himself, but I understood how political some facets of education could be.

I reassured Patrick, I would be very strategic when it came to Mrs. Robertson but he had to let me do my job. I had a very special plan for Mrs. Robertson.

Before we hung up the phone, I had to get some background knowledge on Mr. Jenkins. Patrick stated that Mr. Jenkins was a very good teacher and the students respected him. Mr. Jenkins wore many hats around the school. He was the science teacher, department chair, football coach, and athletic director. He was very flexible and always took on new challenges. I figured that was the reason why Mr. Jenkins was so unorganized. He had plenty on his plate.

The Unorganized
Debriefing

The next morning, I was scheduled to meet Mr. Jenkins in his office. The athletic director's office was located in the gym. It was a small room outside of the boys' locker room. I assumed his office would be quite a mess from his classroom setting, but I was mistaken.

His office was an empty room with a desk, a chair, and a filing cabinet. It looked like it was unoccupied. There was a large sign on the back wall that read, *"No Excuses, Just Results! "*Our meeting was supposed to start at 9:00 a.m., but it was already 9:20 a.m. and Mr. Jenkins was a no show.

When I was packing up my stuff to leave, I heard someone opening the gym door. It was Mr. Jenkins. As usual, he was running late. He was very apologetic for his tardiness and told me the meeting time had slipped his mind. I excused the tardiness and started the meeting. I told him that his class was extraordinary! I enjoyed every minute of it.

I asked Mr. Jenkins to name one thing he thought or wanted me to do for him. Mr. Jenkins replied, "If you could give me a secretary to get my life organized, I would be forever grateful to you." We both started laughing. I told him I couldn't get him a secretary, but I could give him some recommendations for organization.

It was important for Mr. Jenkins to put his priorities in order. Mr. Jenkins wore many hats at the school, and it was vital for him to be on top of all of his affairs. The previous night, I created a three-by-five-foot blank calendar that could be hung from his cabinet. At the top of the calendar, I developed a color-coded system to help Mr. Jenkins organize his day. I told him that he could adapt the color-coded system if needed. A picture of the calendar developed is below:

With the calendar, I gave Mr. Jenkins a set of colored markers to maintain the calendar. Mr. Jenkins was very thankful. I also informed him that I spoke to the principal and requested that he could have half a day to work on his calendar and lesson plans.

I told Mr. Jenkins I was in the process of developing a lesson plan template that would be less time consuming but provided the necessary information required. During his half-day, I would work with him to get his affairs in order. In addition to Mr. Jenkins organizing his calendar and creating lesson plans, I informed Mr. Jenkins of ZipGrade.

ZipGrade is a program where students can write their answers on a bubble sheet and teachers can quickly grade it online quickly by using a iPad or iPhone. Depending on what subscription is purchased, certain data can also be pulled from the program. ZipGrade would be beneficial for Mr. Jenkins. Using the program would decrease the amount of papers he carried around and increase the rate of grading papers. I informed Mr. Jenkins that I would have other technology websites ready for him at our next meeting and he could choose from the list to make his life easier!

Mr. Jenkins was very eager about this arrangement but he still had a unsure look on his face. Before I walked out of his office, I pointed at Mr. Jenkins and directed him to look at his sign: *"No Excuses, Just Results."* He grinned and shook his head.

The International Exchange

Flatter me, and I may not believe you.
Criticize me, and I may not like you. Ignore
me, and I may not forgive you. Encourage
me, and I will not forget you. Love me
and I may be forced to love you.

—William Arthur Ward

Today, I wanted to do things differently than I
had before with the other teachers. I wanted
to meet Mrs. Clemente before I observed her
class to get to know her a little. She was from a

small town in Argentina. She had taught all over the world, and she had over fifteen years of teaching experience before coming to Capers Middle School.

She was a very intelligent woman. You could tell from just holding a conversation with her. This was her first experience teaching at an inner city school. I know this was a cultural shock for her being things are done differently from district to district, state to state, and country to country. I wanted to sit down and talk to her about her teaching experiences previously and how they compare to the teaching experience at Capers Middle School.

Mrs. Clemente was a short woman in stature but walked with the confidence of a ten-foot-tall giant. When she entered the room, she had a look of grace with a pleasant smile. I marveled at how a woman who carried herself so well could have any issues in her classroom. What I learned during my stint in education is even the best of us struggle at some point.

"Mrs. Clemente, how is your school year going?" She looked at me and smiled. She said this year was terrific. She loved the school, the district, and especially the students. I still noticed a look of worry on her face as she spoke though.

I then asked her, "What would be one thing you would change?"

She told me that "I wish that I could just teach and that is it!"

She started to speak about all the different things that were required of her as a teacher and how it frustrated her. She also said sometimes she did not understand why she needed to compete some of the tasks because they were redundant.

While Mrs. Clemente was talking, her eyes became watery. I could tell she had a lot of built-up frustration. She even stated that no one showed her how to complete the tasks or even took the time to check and see if she understood how to complete them. I understood her frustration.

While listening to her concerns, it took me back to my first year of teaching a statistics class at Capers High School. I was a new teacher with no curriculum and no support. The experience was very frustrating, but I knew how to adapt for I was familiar with the culture and the content. Mrs. Clemente did commend Mrs. Robertson (*boastful*) for assisting her at one point. I was surprised and pleased to hear Mrs. Boastful, I mean Mrs. Robertson's name in a positive light. Maybe this was another relationship I could use to my advantage and build on.

Things Were Looking Up

Yesterday is not ours to recover, but
tomorrow is ours to win or lose.

—Lyndon B. Johnson

When I went home for the weekend, I knew I had to develop a plan to assist Mrs. Clemente. I wanted to make her school year less worrisome by finding her a mentor on the staff. As I was contemplating a plan, my phone rang. It was Patrick. We talked about this week and my observations. I told him about some of the issues the five teachers had.

At one point in the conversation, he started laughing and asked if the school had a chance. I told him definitely. He had a good group of teachers. I told him that the list of teachers would become his leadership group for the rest of his staff. He was surprised by that compliment. He told me a parent had called about Mrs. Robertson (boastful). I was shocked—not the superstar! The parent was concerned with the treatment of her son in class. He was failing Mrs. Robertson's class and said that she told him that he didn't stand a chance to pass. She called him a lost cause. For some reason, I wasn't stunned.

During the conversation Mrs. Robertson and I had, I knew that was something she would have said. The parent was threatening to go to the district office. She had notes and e-mails pertaining to her child to receive tutoring. Mrs. Robertson never replied to the e-mails, never sent home progress reports, and never gave the child the opportunity to get help. He assured the parent that he would meet with Mrs. Robertson about her child.

I then asked him, "What did Mrs. Robertson say?"

He stated she acted bewildered about the entire situation. "I told Mrs. Robertson I would fix the situation, but she must meet with you on Monday to figure out ways to support all her students."

I just knew this would not be a good meeting because she was required to attend. I had great intentions for the meeting next week, but after that phone call, anything was liable to happen.

World War III
Meeting

Education is the ability to listen to almost anything without losing your temper or your self-confidence.

—Robert Frost

After a very productive weekend, I was ready to meet with Mrs. Robertson. I knew I had to prepare myself for an interesting but nonproductive meeting. When I arrived at the school, I was met by Ms. Clemente in the parking lot.

"Mr. Gause, after we met on Friday, I went home and made a list of all the difficulties international teachers may encounter. I wanted you to know so you can develop strategies or suggestions that may help us. Please let me know what you come up with. I'm very eager to implement new strategies to be successful."

I looked at the list and told her, "Thanks!"

Ms. Clemente's list read:

- Grading system

- Classroom management

- Overview of students' background

- Language and culture barriers

After reading the list, I was not at all shocked. A lot of times, new teachers share the same struggles. Even though international teachers may come with a lot of experience, they are still new to our educational process and culture in the United States.

After speaking with Mrs. Clemente, I felt good that some of the staff really trusted me. Now if I could get Mrs. Robertson to trust me too, I'd be elated! When I went to sign in at the office, Mrs. Robertson was talking to the secretary. When she saw me, she had the biggest smile on her face.

"Good morning, Mr. Gause. How was your weekend? Is it possible, that we meet this morning?"

Can you say stunned! I was very surprised by the change in Mrs. Robertson's demeanor. I thought I would have to put out an APB just to meet with her. "Yes, we can most definitely meet," I replied.

We walked down to her room. When we sat down, she told me about the meeting she had with the parent. She told me that she never had anyone want to go to the district office about her before.

She didn't want her reputation tarnished by the situation, so she was willing and ready to listen and implement any suggestions I had. I asked if she tried to give the parent's child any responsibility. When I was in her class observing, I noticed that Mrs. Robertson had student leaders and classroom ambassadors.

She said, "No, the student is lazy."

As teachers, we have to set standards for our students. It does not matter if they're lazy; we have to push them. I advised her to allow him to be the material manager. He would be responsible to pass out any resources needed for the class. Also, I asked her what some of the student's interests were. She stated that he always talked about Jordans and Kevin Durant tennis shoes.

Since her class was English, I suggested she find different books, articles, blogs, or magazines for him to read that piqued his interest. She could tweak her lesson a little for him, so she could reach every child. Every student deserves the same quality education no matter his or her shortcomings. As teachers we must *push*!

Mrs. Robertson was actually writing down my suggestions. I felt a nice sense of accomplishment finally reaching Mrs. Robertson. She said she would try these two ideas and see if there were any changes with the student. When I was about to leave the class, I remembered Ms. Clemente's list.

"Could you do me a favor?" I asked Mrs. Robertson.

She said, "Yes."

I asked if she could be a mentor to Mrs. Clemente. She asked, "What does being a mentor mean? Is that a lot of work?"

She smiled and stated she was playing. I told her I just wanted her to check on Mrs. Clemente three times a week. The meetings would be informal and would serve as a quick check to see if Mrs. Clemente was having any difficulties and to possibly assist her with them. I wanted her to be someone Mrs. Clemente could confide in. She said she would do it. I left the meeting very pleased.

Observing the Obvious

The mediocre teacher tells. The good teacher explains. The superior teacher demonstrates. The great teacher inspires.

—William Arthur Ward

Over the next two weeks, I wanted to see how my recommendations were coming along and if any of the teachers had implemented the strategies. For teachers or people in any profession to perfect their craft, they will need to practice, research, read, and use other various ways to continue learning so they can stay current. On the way to observe Ms. Simpson's class, I happened to walk past the teachers' lounge. I could hear some teachers talking about updating their grades in PowerSchool.

It was Mrs. Clemente, Mr. Rodriguez, and Mrs. Robertson. When I opened the door, Mrs. Robertson turned around. We look at each other, and I gave her a wink and nodded my head in appreciation. With a glowing smile on her face, Mrs. Clemente saw me and invited me to come inside. When I entered the lounge, Mrs. Robertson was on her way out. She reached out her hand to me for a fist pump. I was confused by the gesture. She said she wanted to just thank me for helping her with the situation with the student. Mrs. Clemente was standing by the copy machine.

She said, "Hey, Mr. Gause. How are you doing? I don't know if you spoke to Mrs. Robertson, but she has been a great help to me and the other international teachers. She basically helps me with all the schools nonnegotiables, and I pass on my learning to the rest of the international teachers. She calls me at least two to three times a week to check on me. I feel more comfortable working at Capers Middle."

I replied, "The best gift of them all is giving. I am glad that you all are working together as a team. Mrs. Robertson is your support, and you are the other international teachers' support."

After talking to Mrs. Clemente, I continued my walk to Ms. Simpson's class. When I arrived at the seventh-grade hall, I saw a flyer for a new student and teacher mentor group. The facilitators of mentor group were Ms. Simpson and Mrs. Humphrey. Having a mentor group is a great way for teachers to build relationships with the students. Through relationship building, one can overcome many obstacles that present themselves to students and teachers both inside and outside of the classroom.

To teach children, you must first reach them. Through this mentor group, many successes would be made toward Ms. Simpson's classroom management issues and Mrs. Robertson's student engagement.

When I walked into Ms. Simpson's classroom, it was different from the initial observation. Her class was not as loud and rambunctious as before. The students were working in groups and actually talking about the assignment. Cue cards were made for each group to foster meaningful dialogue. The students were engaged in conversation.

At one point during the group collaboration, two students started playing with pencils and were off task. Ms. Simpson started counting, "One, two, three." The group the off-task students were a part of looked at their peers and corrected their behavior. Ms. Simpson stopped the count and continued to informally assess the other groups. I was very impressed. Ms. Simpson allowed the students to correct each other's behavior and hold their classmates accountable, allowing the class to create a respectful learning community. She did not become frustrated or even embarrass the students by directly correcting the students. She used a counting technique and allowed the students to correct themselves.

After I witnessed how she handled the situation, I made my way out the class and down the hallway. My next stop on today's agenda was to visit Mr. Jenkins.

While I was walking toward Mr. Jenkins's classroom, the bell rang. I had to maneuver through the miniature people called students in the hallway. While maneuvering through the crowd, who came racing past me like a flash of lightning? It was Mr. Jenkins. He was racing to get to his classroom. I quickly thought to myself, *I just know that Mr. Jenkins didn't implement any of my ideas.* Mr. Jenkins running to his classroom was deja vu.

When I arrived at his classroom, I expected Mr. Jenkins to be unorganized. I was shocked to see just the opposite. Mr. Jenkins had an agenda, the current standard, and the essential question on the board. They daily activities were listed. This was a complete turnaround from three weeks ago. Mr. Jenkins walked over to me and pointed at his cabinet. He had a thirty-one-day calendar taped to the front of his cabinet. The different dates and times were color coordinated.

Mr. Jenkins told me he still had a long way to go, but he was proud that he was making an effort to be organized. I stayed in the class for the remainder of the period. I was very impressed by how Mr. Jenkins transitioned from one activity to the next and was able to get to all his activities before the end of the class.

His timing was remarkable! I liked the timer he placed on the smart board so the students would be aware of the timing. I gave Mr. Jenkins a thumbs-up and left his room. Small improvements in the classroom can totally turn around the flow. It is important for teachers to have a plan for every aspect, from sharpening pencils to leaving their seats.

After observing Mr. Jenkins and Ms. Simpson, I went to see Mrs. Humphrey. Before I could get to Mrs. Humphrey's class, Patrick stopped me in the hallway. He wanted a quick update on the teachers. I told him that everything was looking very good. The teachers were collaborating with each other, and they were implementing some of my ideas. We spoke for about twenty minutes, and I continued my journey to Mrs. Humphrey's class. I arrived about fifteen minutes before the bell was about ring. When I reached for the door, I heard the students clapping and cheering. I had to look at the number on the door to make sure I was entering the right room. When I walked in the room, the students were playing Kahoot It. Kahoot It is an free online question competition game. Teachers can input questions and answers in the application or choose predesigned games created by other teachers, and the students play the game individually, as a whole class, or on teams. Students use their laptops or any device with Internet access to play the game. Kahoot can be used to assess or review any standard. Mrs. Humphrey was using the online application as a closing activity. The students were very engaged.

This was a totally different atmosphere than three weeks ago. Mrs. Humphrey was using technology, and the students were engrossed in the activity. After I left Mrs. Humphrey's class, I ended my day. I went home to write up notes about the observations so I could debrief with the teachers tomorrow.

Since yesterday was so illuminating, I was ready to get my day started at Capers Middle. It was a delayed start at the school for students, so Patrick scheduled a faculty meeting. I wanted to see if there would be a difference from the first faculty meeting I attended. There were some slight differences. Patrick told the teachers to break up into groups and look over the second nine weeks data. Mrs. Robertson joined the group with Mrs. Clemente and the other international teachers. She was showing them how to break down the data. Mrs. Humphrey and Ms. Simpson also formed a group with two other teachers. Mr. Jenkins did not attend the meeting. He had to attend a district meeting for coaches. I still noted that some staff members didn't take the data seriously. One group didn't even look at the data. One member said the data had been the same for the last five years. She didn't see the use of analyzing it.

From the meeting, I knew it was time for me to get the *defective five* together to change the atmosphere of the entire school. My only question was, "Will the *defective five* be able to work together to change the *dysfunctional staff*?"

I met with Patrick to discuss my plan to help change the climate of the school. I told him for his school to move forward, we had to implement the five big Cs. The five big Cs was a formula I developed to change the culture of a school. It all started when I assisted Capers Elementary's Staff. The school was falling apart because morale was very low and there was no sense of community. Patrick asked what were the big Cs. The big Cs are culture, communication, character, collaboration (creativity), and commitment (consistency). I stated the only way the big Cs could be implemented successfully is if we had full commitment from the staff.

Since I had built a relationship with the defective five, they were the perfect ones to introduce the big Cs to the staff. I actually used this formula to get them going so they would know the ropes.

The Plan

Alone we can do so little; together
we can do so much.

—Helen Keller

Patrick called Mrs. Robertson, Ms. Humphrey, Mr. Jenkins, Ms. Simpson, and Ms. Clemente to the professional development room. To my surprise, Mr. Jenkins was the first person through the door. Then came Ms. Simpson and Ms. Humphrey. Last entered Mrs. Robertson and Ms. Clemente. They were laughing and talking. This was not the group I saw at the first faculty meeting.

Patrick told the group that he had a big task for them. He told them he needed them for a special assignment and I would elaborate more about it. While Patrick was speaking, I examined the group's body language. They looked attentive and excited. I gave each of them a card with one of the big Cs. Mrs. Robertson received the *character* card. Mr. Jenkins's card had the word *consistency/commitment*. Ms. Clemente's card read *communication*. Ms. Simpson started smiling because her card was *collaboration/ creativity*, and Mrs. Humphrey's card had the word *culture* written on it. I told each of the teachers to tell each other the word on their cards and explain what it meant to them in their own words regarding education.

To say the least, it was a very interesting conversation. At the end of the conversation, the group came to the consensus that each of the words connected to one another. Ms. Simpson explained to be a successful person in any facet of life, you have to have all of these characteristics.

After the teachers discussed their cards, I chimed in. "I would like each of you to host a professional development based on your card. For the next five half-days of the school year, each of you all will be doing a forty-five-minute mini session on your characteristics."

Each of them looked at each other with confusion. The newbie teacher said she was too new to do a professional development. I told her sometimes a new voice is just what some staff members needed to hear. Coach Jenkins looked around and stated that he was just getting his stuff together. He didn't have time to come up with a professional development. That would take a lot of work. Mrs. Robertson stated no one really liked her so no one would come to see her. I listened to them for about five minutes.

I stopped them and told them to relax. "I gave each of you a particular card because that was your strongest trait."

I told them if they worked together, the task of creating a professional development wouldn't be hard. For example, Mrs. Robertson thought the highest of herself, so she would be able to talk about character for hours. I told Mrs. Clemente that she would be the best for communication because that was a major factor in her being more successful in her class and among her coworkers. Mr. Jenkins stated he had could help with consistency because that was his weakness, but now that he was organized, it was his strength.

Ms. Simpson said, "We need a catchy title for each of our sessions."

Mrs. Clemente said, "Let's call the mini sessions food for thought. Each of us can bring a dish as an appetizer for the attendees to eat while they are in our sessions."

Everyone liked the idea. Now, we had to develop some creative names for each of the mini sessions. These are the names that the defective five developed: Negative Nancy (culture), Money

Talks (communication), Lifestyles (character), Dream Car (creativity/collaboration), and Play Your Part (commitment/consistency). Over the next four hours, we worked together to develop some engaging activities that would help us meet our goal of changing the culture of the school.

Food for Thought

I am great but through collaboration and communication with my peer, I will become

Greater and with trust and commitment of this family, we will be the

Greatest.

—Alvin Allen

On the first half-day, I visited the school to view each of the mini sessions. Over the next five half-days, each staff member at

Capers Middle had to participate in all the mini sessions. Each session would hold up to twenty-five staff members. Since Ms. Simpson was the newbie of the staff, I wanted to visit her mini conference first. Her conference was named, "Dream Car." Her overall goal was to promote creativity and show the staff how creativity promotes collaboration and communication. She had about twenty teachers in her session. At the front of the classroom, she had a variety of food. Each food item had a price tag with it.

For example, there were donuts for fifty dollars each, cookies for forty dollars each, hotdog buns for five hundred dollars each, and other items. The teachers were set up in groups of four. Each group had a handout with a list of directions, sketchbook, calculator, and a worksheet. Also, they had name tags with different job titles. There was an engineer, accountant, artist, and quality tester. Each group's main objective was to build a race car out of different food items. Their car would be judged on design, cost efficiency, and distance of travel in ten seconds. Each group had thirty minutes to draw and build their cars. The teachers were so engaged and were very creative in their design. They communicated and collaborated so well together.

It was a lot of laughing and joking, but everyone worked diligently. I stepped out before the end, but the goal was accomplished. The teachers were be creative through collaboration and communication.

Next, I visited Mrs. Humphrey. Her mini conference pertained to culture. It was called "Negative Nancy." She wanted everyone to understand the importance of working as a team and not letting negativity destroy the culture of the school. There were twenty-eight teachers in her session. She had previously talked to three teachers before the meeting and she asked them to be negative throughout her presentation.

When I walked in the room, I heard a teacher say, "I am tired of seeing that man. He can't fix this dumb school."

Someone tapped him and said, "Stop being so negative."

The class was split into two halves. They were fourteen teachers on each side of the room. They were discussing a news article about the democratic and republican parties. They were debating different sections of the article and had to make a stand depending on the side of class. Throughout the activity, the three teachers were very negative of everything. It got to the point that the teachers were pushing them out the groups.

Once the activity was over, Ms. Richards asked, "Why did those three come to your session?"

I am going to call them the session killers. Mrs. Humphrey told three teachers thank you and let the group know she asked them to be negative prior to the session. Her next step was to discuss how negativity can be a major factor in stopping school improvement. While she was going into her activity, I smiled at Mrs. Humphrey and walked out the room.

The next session I visited was, "Money Talks." Mrs. Clemente was in charge of this mini conference. When I walked in the room, there was a great aroma. She had cooked a Spanish dish from her home country. The bowl was almost empty. I noticed some of the teachers had fake dollar bills on their desks. On the board, she had the directions for using the dollar bills. Each teacher was given three different bills—a one, a five, and a ten-dollar bill. The one-dollar bill was to make a statement (short answer). The five-dollar bill was to ask a question, and the ten-dollar bill was to participate in meaningful dialogue during the session. The goal was to not have any money at end of the session. The teachers who did not have any money at the end of the session were eligible to win a door prize.

I was elated about the session because the goal was to promote communication among the staff, and the activity encouraged input from everyone. After going to three sessions, I was geared up to see the last two sessions, but time would not permit. I met with the five defective teachers after their presentations. Each of them had the attendees do evaluations from their presentations.

I read the evaluations. The teachers really liked their presentations and came away with a new perspective for the school year. I was proud of them, and I let them know. I told them I would come back on the next half day to observe Mr. Jenkins and Mrs. Robertson.

Even though a month had gone by since I visited Capers Middle, I stayed in contact with Patrick to ensure he was doing something to keep the positive culture and morale up at his school. He said the staff was doing better. He said he could see that the school atmosphere was changing. I was ready to see for myself.

When the next half day came, I couldn't wait to visit the last two teachers' mini sessions. When I entered Mrs. Robertson's classroom, the teachers were sitting at the desk eating some fried chicken. Everyone knew Mrs. Robertson could cook some good fried chicken. While they were eating, Mrs. Robertson had them fill out a characteristic survey. Once everyone had finished their survey and food, she told them to read the directions at the bottom of the survey and calculate the total. Then she directed them to stand in the middle of the classroom. In the four corners of the room, there were four different cars. There was a Mercedes, a van, a Lamborghini, and a Honda. She stated that if their numbers added up between twenty and twenty-four to stand by the van, twenty and twenty-nine to stand by the Mercedes, thirty and thirty-four to stand by the Honda, and thirty-five to thirty-nine to stand by the Lamborghini. Some of the teachers were picking at the other teachers for standing by the minivans. One teacher said she could pay for her van but they would be living out of their car trying to pay for a Lamborghini on a teacher's salary. They were laughing and joking. Mrs. Robertson told them to think more about the characteristics of the car and discuss why they thought their characteristics modeled that particular type of car. After each group chimed in, they discussed what each group had in common. The main characteristic of the minivan was its dependability. The Lamborghini was nice looking, so they related that to being organized in the teacher world and on time to make a good appearance. While they were in their discussion, I walked over to Mrs. Robertson and told her she had done a great job. After their open discussion, they started to discuss how members from the different car groups should be on teams because they all offered different characteristics that can help reach goals and be successful. Last but not least, it was time to visit Mr. Jenkins. Mr. Jenkins's mini conference pertained to commitment and consistency. The name of it was, "Play Your Part". Mr. Jenkins had various costumes in the center of the classroom. There were about thirty people in his conference. He told them to break out in groups of five. Each group had to create a skit showing commitment or consistency in different careers. He handed each group a different sheet of paper with a career field. The different career fields were business, circus, music, bakery, and farming. Each group had twenty minutes to dress up and create a skit that portrayed one of the characteristics. I stayed around to listen to the groups.

The first group came up to the front. They had to show commitment in the circus. Three of the teachers were dressed like clowns, and the last two were dressed liked mimes. The mimes pointed at the desk and told the three clowns to fit in it. It was so hilarious seeing them trying to fit into one desk and the mimes telling them ideas through sign language. They tried at least eight different ways to get in the desk, but they never gave up until they accomplished their task.

After their accomplishment, one of the teachers held up a sign that said, "If you never give up, that shows commitment." Everyone laughed so hard. All I could say was goal accomplished. I was so proud of Mr. Jenkins. I left before the other groups demonstrated their skits, but I knew they would be good as well. Mr. Jenkins videotaped the skits and put it on the school flash drive for everyone's enjoyment.

I went to Patrick's office. He was talking to the curriculum resource teacher. She said the mini conferences were the best professional development the school had in years. The most important thing was that they were all led by one of their own staff members. Patrick said he knew after teachers had visited each of the sessions, they would get a clear picture of the new culture and expectations of the school.

His plan was to have a staff meeting and develop three main standards for the staff to build a foundation for years to come. I shook Mr. Patrick's hand and told him to call me if he needed any more help. When I walked out the school, the sun was shining bright. I was smiling ear to ear. I had played a major role in remodeling the culture of the school so students could receive A1 education daily.

Teaching Strategies

Listed below are some strategies used in the book by the teachers that you can use in your classroom!

The Unorganized Teacher

- Daily agenda

- Color-coded calendar

- Transitions timer

Alvin Allen; Dominique Bennett

The International Teacher

- Buddy

- Student entrance survey

- About the teacher presentation

The Veteran Teacher

- Class flow

- Kahoot

- Operation:_(Topic Here)____

  For more details and directions about activities, contact us by e-mail: *llegacyed@gmail.com*

The Boastful Teacher

- Classroom ambassadors

- Family tree (Building classroom community and everyone is important)

- Quick pick (Student engagement)

The Newbie Teacher

- Musical chairs (*have music playing and the students pick the number for class seating arrangement*)

- Mentor

- Closing activity: sink and swim

> For more details and directions about activities, contact us by e-mail: *llegacyed@gmail.com*

Author Biography

Alvin Allen has been working in the esteemed school district of Richland One in Columbia, South Carolina, since 2006. He is currently a math facilitator and STEAM coordinator for W. A. Perry Middle School. Most of his career in Richland One has been geared toward helping inner city youth. He has worked diligently in two of the district's former priority schools. He has a master's in educational technology from Webster University and is currently working on his education specialist degree in technology leadership. In his thirteen-year teaching career, he has been voted twice as teacher of the year by his colleagues. He has also received the Instructional Technology Spotlight Award by the district for his usage of technology to differentiate instruction. For the last seven years, his Algebra I students have earned a 100 percent passing rate with an overall 91 average on the end of course state examination. Mr. Allen has served on many school and district committees to help to improve student achievement throughout his career.

He has self-published a trilogy of books *Capers Middle School, Capers Middle School II: The Saga Continues,* and *Capers Middle School III: Life Is Not a Fairytale.* The trilogy focuses on building relationships with students and the struggles students face in today's schools.

Mr. Allen is cofounder of an educational consulting company called iLEGACY (integrating and leading educator in grooming and cultivating youth). His company has presented on the issue of engaging students in the classroom at several educational conferences in South Carolina and Georgia. Mr. Allen believes that all students, no matter their ethnic background or circumstances, are reachable and teachable.

Dominique Bennett is a product of the Richland County School District One school system. She attended the University of South Carolina, in Columbia, where she earned her bachelor's degree in Middle Level Education with a focus in Mathematics and Social Studies. She then attended the University of Phoenix where she earned her Master's degree in Early Childhood Education. Dominique is currently pursuing a Doctors in Education with a focus in Curriculum and Instruction.

Dominique has been teaching for four years for Richland County School District One. She works in the inner city with students from low socio-economic back grounds. She is a middle school mathematics teacher. She is also the co-author of *The 5 Defective Teachers and Staff.* Dominique has three children, two girls and a boy. They reside in Columbia, S.C.

Dominique believes that education is a key to success. Teachers and scholars can be successful with the right tools. Dominique enjoys helping young scholars thrive to be prosperous citizens. She also enjoys sharing her knowledge with teachers to help teachers perfect their craft.